Waiting for the Gulf Stream

for Adi, who is also waiting for the Gulf Stream,
all good wishes,
Bert
Kyoto, April 6, 2013

Waiting for the Gulf Stream

Bert Almon

HAGIOS PRESS
Box 33024 Cathedral PO
Regina SK S4T 7X2
www.hagiospress.com

Copyright © 2010 Bert Almon

All rights reserved. No part of this publication may be reproduced, stored in a retrieval system, or transmitted in any form or by any means without the prior written permission of the publisher or by licensed agreement with Access: The Canadian Copyright Licensing Agency. Exceptions will be made in the case of a reviewer, who may quote brief passages in a review to print in a magazine or newspaper, broadcast on radio or television, or post on the Internet.

Library and Archives Canada Cataloguing in Publication

Almon, Bert, 1943–
  Waiting for the Gulf Stream / Bert Almon.

Poems.
ISBN 978-1-926710-08-2

  1. Title

PS8551.L58W35 2010   C811'.54   C2010-905553-5

Edited by Alan Safarik.
Cover design by Tania Wolk.
Cover Art by Ian Rawlinson.
Designed and typeset by Donald Ward.
Set in Adobe Caslon Pro.
Printed and bound in Canada.
Text pages printed on:

Mixed Sources
Cert no. SW-COC-001271
© 1996 FSC

Hagios Press gratefully acknowledges support for the production of this book as provided by:

  Canada Council for the Arts   Conseil des Arts du Canada

For more information on Hagios Press and our books see
www.hagiospress.com

for Olga

Contents

A Model Close at Hand	11
Inclusions in Books	12
Clint	13
Talking about Poetry at the Local Jail	15
Identities	16
Our Lady of Peace	18
Game Room, Extendacare Centre	19
Bright Shadows	20
The Cracking Tower	22
The Lineman	24
Grand Texas Minuet	25
Saturday Lessons	27
My Mother's Possum	28
It Stands to Reason	30
Shoofly Pie	31
Beverly Ann Lee (1936-2006)	32
In Praise of Gravy	34
Did You Ever See Such a Sight	35
Bed and Breakfast	36
A Duty of Care	37
The Firebrand River	39
The Gang	41
Scenes Glimpsed through a BritRail Sandwich	42
Driving around Cape Sable Island	44
A Celestial Symposium	45
Walter Benjamin Checks into the Kaanapali Hyatt-Regency	46
A Partial Tour Guide to West Edmonton Mall	47
More Fun than a Barrel of Sea-Monkeys	49

Uncle Ned Says Grace	50
Reading the Entrails	51
Scenes from a Divorce	53
The Eyewitness	55
The Passionate Haystack	56
Three Birdsongs	57
Hawthornden Hours	59
Bombay Sapphire	60
Portobello Road Market	61
Venus in Edinburgh	62
The French Bed	64
Aelbert Cuyp: River Landscape with Horseman and Peasants	65
The Art of Painting	66
Entering Paradise	67
Treasures of the Green Vault. Dresden	68
The Demonstrators	70
Wedding Cakes and Buddhas	72
The Lorelei	74
Unfinished Symphony	75
Jessica Williams at the Yardbird Suite	77
Aboard the Twin Star Rocket	78
Astral Journey	79
Along the Queen Elizabeth II Highway	80
Open Books	81
Eastern Pennsylvania on Flag Day	82
Days of -39	84
Zones of Hardiness	85

Waiting for the Gulf Stream

A Model Close at Hand

for Margy Forbis

After living ninety years, she tells us
she has the simplest theology:
there is a plus at the heart of things,
a simple plus. I think right away
of entropy's steady abrasions,
and of the evil in the world, but a little later
she says that she can only watch
the news hour while knitting clothes
for premature babies. The act
of pulling stitches of bright yarn
through each other adds a vertical stroke
to the thick minus sign
of world events. The neonatal wards
want all the knitted caps they can get.
A preemie's head is about
the size of an orange or sometimes a lemon,
and a model is always close at hand.

Inclusions in Books

for Don Domanski

In an archive I found a dried Cherokee Rose
pressed between the pages of a rare book
about the Trail of Tears. The librarian
sealed the flower in plastic with a note
and placed it in a file folder marked "Ephemera."
In Cincinnati volunteers sorting old books
for a charity sale found elm leaves, uncashed cheques,
a 45 rpm disk by the East Side Kids
called "Chocolate Matzos," a pair of 3D glasses,
and even a petrified strip of bacon.
And there are the inscriptions on flyleaves,
loving or formal. Dealers put a premium
on the admiring message by one author
written in great looping letters
to another, who peddled it right away.

What to make of the book I bought second hand,
poems called *Heaven*, with the inscription:

    Love Me. ♥
    Nov. 29/88
    3rd year.

I want to restore these phantoms and bring them
to a racing pulse of love, but I stand baffled,
an ER Cupid who can't find his patients,
holding the paddles of the defibrillator.
Was the book lost, or stolen, or sold in anger?
Why *Love Me* and not *Love You*?
Or did the writer mean *Love, Me*, forgetting the comma?
Third year? Of what, of how many?

Clint

Clint's poems survive only
in his explanations of them.
There was the break-through poem,
that shocked his writing class:
"I realized last night that being a native
doesn't mean I have to write about buffalo
or how we got the Sacred Pipe.
It's about speeding down Highway 2
with a bottle between my legs and the windows down,
rock-and-roll blasting on the radio."
And I don't have a copy of the poem
with the mysterious reference
to Atthis and Sappho, which he glossed this way:
"I used those names because if I had breasts,
I'd name the left one Sappho
and the right one Atthis."
I remember his pose of admiring Jeffrey Dahmer,
and his plan to become a clinical psychologist,
for which his sole qualification
was a complete scrapbook of *Penthouse Forum*.

He was a whole encampment
of camp figures.
Like Sappho, he jumped to his death,
a bridge was his Aegean cliff.
She left fragments of poetry,
Clint left his asides and his surprise exit.
We still expect him to step out of a curtain
somewhere and take a bow.

Ship Models

for Bill Forbis

Bill has a fleet of model ships under glass:
safe from storms and shipwreck.
He's built the schooner-yacht *America*,
in its slender elegance. Special for him
is the *Wolverine*, one of the freighters built
on Hog Island in Philadelphia.
He sailed on the real *Wolverine* in World War II.
The model of the *Star of India*, the oldest sailing ship
in service, looks flawless to me. At a model-builder's show
the experts offered to give him their opinion
for fifteen dollars. They said that it was a good likeness —
at a distance of six feet. During the war,
the ship just ahead of *The Wolverine* in the convoy
was sunk by a torpedo. That was close enough, he says.

Talking about Poetry at the Local Jail

This was a minimum security pen
but I got to wear a plastic id card
clipped to my shirt pocket
It said "writer"   my first certification
of that vagrant status
I visited a classroom in the basement
Four students were wearing hospital gowns
"Baby dolls" such prisoners are called
the ones who might set themselves on fire
The gowns are soaked in fire-retardant
The teacher described the uproar
when a pupil bursts into flame
in the middle of a lesson
The Promethean metaphors for learning
self-destruct in such an atmosphere
Better to light one candle
Kindling enthusiasm
Passing the torch
Setting the world on fire

The serious poets were all
in the protective custody wing
The informants and sex offenders

Identities

1. *London Accent*

When I figured out what the poster
meant by Identity Parade, I went
to the police station to volunteer.
I was a good generic crypto-criminal,
medium height, brown hair,
no distinguishing marks or features.
I could stand under sweating lights
with the other volunteers, and the suspect,
and try to look tough, or try to look
like a tough guy pretending to be meek.
The bobbie at the desk laughed, explained
that I'd need to say, "Give me your wallet,
you sod," in an East End accent.

2. *The London Letter*

When someone forged a cheque
in the husband's name, the rancher and his wife
had to sit down with the Mountie
and copy out The "London Letter,"
a dull text designed to give samples
of all letters and combinations,
all the loops, crosses and ligatures,
a way to tell if the wife had tried
to imitate her husband's signature
or if he'd tried to disguise his own.
The four year old child watching
never forgot her parents sitting
across from each other at the kitchen table,
with the detective at right angles to them.
The husband, with his three years

of schooling, wrote slowly,
slowly. The Mountie tapped the table
with his fingers, grew more suspicious.
The innocent were made to feel guilty,
the unschooled man's humiliation
simulating a bad conscience.

3. *A Stroke of Ink*

At the checkout, the woman
waved the plastic divider at me
and asked where it belonged,
where her groceries ended
and mine started. It was all swept together
by the speed of the conveyor belt.
She had a trace of accent
and her dyed hair made her look
just a little older than me.
I was stopped dead
when I saw the tattoo on her arm,
a row of black numbers. The seven
was in continental style, a little bar
across the stem, a short stroke of the needle.

Our Lady of Peace

Dunvegan, Peace River Valley

She's twice my height and wears
a marble crown on her marble head.
She is too serene to notice the 27-speed bike
leaning against her side,
or the serpent at her feet.
The apple in his mouth is the world,
and he is choking on it.

She has never tasted sin.

On the bike trails behind the statue,
two Old Colony Mennonite girls
in long blue dresses are doing stunts
on their heavy one-speeds,
whooping with laughter behind the Virgin's back,
eager for the taste of apple.

Game Room, Extendacare Centre

No one picks up the cards, board games
rest in the box. Only Daisy is active,
working on her puzzle at a card table:
"Undersea Aliens": cartoon figures
with antennae and eyes on stalks
cruising the sea bottom in UFOs.

Time is what the very old suffer,
not the shortness of the time left,
but the tedium, a heavy afghan
settled on their shoulders as they sit
in the deep chairs of the game room,
most of them women, their hair
gone past grey to cotton white.

Over in the real aquarium, a fish
bumping the glass shines with colours
like a rainbow crushed into sequins,
its thin shape a trapezoid
squeezed into an oval form.
Now it swims by the blind lighthouse,
and around the wrecked galleon.
Tiny coins have spilt from a treasure chest.

Mr. Nehring of 9B passes through,
one foot laboring with the pedal
of his reclining wheelchair: nothing
so slowly, ever-so-slowly, nothing.
The gap in Daisy's puzzle fills in
from the edges. The room sinks
into the plush of silence
till a visitor raps the glass
of the aquarium. The iridescent fish
takes shelter behind the lighthouse.

Bright Shadows

It was unmentionable
that our kindly neighbor Mr. Martinez —
the unemployed musician
briefly employed as a garbage man —
had died under the blade
of the garbage truck
But who could think of anything else?
The revulsion was so great —
the human being crushed with garbage

In the cemetery
he was restored as a musician
the nimble trumpet player
of everyone's memory:
a brass band from Mexico appeared
a tribute from the musician's union
We stood in the desert sun
as they unpacked gleaming instruments
to play the two national anthems
and Chopin's funeral march
— which I had never heard
except as a travesty in the cartoons
something for the burial of an insect —
I was astonished by its gravity

The musicians stood at attention
in brown uniforms with smart caps and visors
their instruments so polished
that sharp flashes of sunlight
flickered over us all

Bright shadows I thought
but I knew they weren't shadows
Some other principle
I couldn't remember the word

After the casket sank into the grave
the band began putting their instruments away
every dismantled part
nestled in its velvet hollow

I kept thinking   *bright shadows*
as the first clods hit the lid of the coffin

The Cracking Tower

My father never took me beyond the gatehouse
where he picked up his paycheque
No one could get in without a badge
I didn't know what it meant to punch the clock
and looked for dents in it
He rose from the bullgang to controlman
a slippery ladder of seniority and merit

One day he drew me a diagram
of the fractionating tower
with its gradient of temperatures
declining with the height of the tower
He sketched in pencil the way
the different vapors are siphoned off
as each finds its thermal level
lubricating oil at 300 C
kerosene at 270
naphtha at 200
and the supreme essence
gasoline at 160

Over the years he was distilled himself
by a gradient of agonies
a heart attack cast out strength a mad wife cast out joy
an estranged son cast out pride
daily angina cast out hope

If suffering has any meaning
these qualities were not lost
When he made his last ride
to find death waiting for his arrival
some essence must have been distilled
but I don't know how it was drawn off
or what place it might have
in the economy of the universe

The Lineman

After a second partner died on a power pole
he broke down completely, hearing radio broadcasts
with the news of the future in currents
that moved through his rubber gauntlets to somewhere
inside his head. The doctors prescribed electroshock:
how could he work on the poles after that? The radio
kept playing, turned down too low for him
to understand anything. He became a maritime guard
and patrolled the docks with a gun and flashlight,
trying to ignore the gabbling voices. After his heart attack,
the volume must have increased again. He was walking
the hospital corridor with his wife. He stopped.
Fearful, she asked him, "What's wrong, Jack?"
He answered, "You'll soon find out," and fell to the floor,
crumpled at the base of a pole no one could see.

Grand Texas Minuet

If the heart has strings
they should be played with fingertips
or the soft stroke of a horsehair bow

At a friend's house over dinner
he said, "I'll bet you remember this"
and put on a Hank Williams record
I remembered every word
All those songs my mother used to play
on yellow-labeled EPs from the Record Corral
The heart shouldn't be plucked with a plastic pick

When I was eight years old
I saw Hank Williams live
A skinny young man in a shirt
with snaps and fringes
He was drunk for an audience
that came to see him drunk
He made them cheer by singing "Jambalaya"
with its happy words to a sad melody
stolen from the Cajun song "Grand Texas"
Dying young couldn't make him Mozart

This was not the music we danced to at school
The sprightly minuet with sadness
underlying its merriment
Awkward boys and bashful girls
drew together with the girl turning
under the boy's hand

A curtsy and a bow ended the ordeal
Many years later at the opera I recognized
Don Giovanni's seductive little minuet
played on a single violin
The music curtsied and I bowed

Saturday Lessons

I was spared the Boy Scouts
when my parents learned the troop
was sponsored by a local brewery:
they could imagine me in shorts drinking beer
around a campfire in the Piney Woods.

I was spared learning the accordion
because the teacher was baffled
by left-handedness and thought
I'd have to hold it upside down.
But it would have been great fun
to play the squeezebox
at the National Jamboree,
maybe worth a merit badge.

I spent Saturdays at the kids' matinees,
watching Tarzan, Bugs Bunny, and scratchy serials
where Buck Rogers flew a rocket ship
that sounded like an outboard motor.
What do I remember best? Hopalong Cassidy
daring to ask for sarsaparilla in a saloon,
and the sneering galoot who threw the first punch.
Hoppy must have had the merit badges
for sobriety and bar-fighting.

My parents never got me the Hopalong Cassidy Rollfast Bicycle,
the one with the handlebars that looked like steer horns.

My Mother's Possum

Night after night I lay insomniac
on the sofa-bed in my mother's front room,
nothing to soothe me to sleep except
jazz on the campus radio, or the horror movies
hosted by Elvira, Mistress of the Dark,
a woman with lips as bright as blood,
and two zeppelins straining almost free
of her neckline. My dying mother
slept in the front bedroom. She complained
about nightly marauding by a possum,
said that it knocked her tooth-glass over,
and ate the Wonder Bread on the kitchen counter.

All through my childhood she was the little girl
who cried *burglar*, slipping into my room
and propping a chair against the doorknob
till the police arrived and said "It's okay, ma'am"
over and over, with head-shaking patience.

I woke around dawn to the radio buzzing static
and the uproar in the kitchen: bottles rolling,
a chair toppling, and some genteel cursing.
I found her by the back door,
holding the lid over a plastic trash bucket:
"I caught him — you have to get rid of him.
But don't hurt him — take this out somewhere
and dump it." I knew there was nothing to dump,
but I put the heavy bucket in the car,
playing a charade of obedience. Five miles later,
I pulled off on the county road to the gates
of a graveyard bright with plastic flowers.
Laying the bucket on its side, I took off the lid.
An enormous brown rat crawled out,

moving slowly, setting off into a grassy ditch.
Fearless, it looked back at my shocked face,
then moved off, its tail dragging
through the dew which the grass blades
would offer up to the advancing sun.
When I got back to Beaux-Arts Garden Road, I said,
"Yes, mother, I got rid of him —
No, mother, I didn't hurt him, not a whisker" —
ma'aming her as well as any weary policeman.

It Stands to Reason

When my parents converted to their odd religion
and learned that Christmas was a pagan holiday,
they took the gifts back to the stores
and threw out the tree, ornaments and all.
Then they sat six-year-old me down to talk about Santa.
My father said, "Does it stand to reason
that one man in an airplane could deliver presents
to every house in the world?" I admire that now,
the argument that killed the magic by substituting
a plane for a sleigh. We didn't even have to discuss
the oddity of levitation in a chimney.
Bits of tinsel would surface in the rug
for months– the vacuum couldn't suck them up.

When my new Sunday School teacher
told us about the loaves and fishes,
I just had a knowing smile:
the death of one miracle is the death of all.

Shoofly Pie

Imagine a cafeteria kitchen
filled with children and clouds of flour,
boys waving rolling pins like clubs,
girls stirring up ingredients in big bowls.
The story in our fifth grade reader
made us long to try the frontier recipe:
molasses, butter and soda
under crumbs of flour, butter and sugar.
It was winter and I was disappointed
there would be no flies to chase away.

But the boys hovered near Betty,
whose precocious nipples showed
under her blouse. We were more disturbed
than aroused by this mark of difference.
Barry had seen the 3-D movie,
"The Creature from the Black Lagoon"
and claimed that the monster,
with its King Kong lineage,
had picked the heroine "up by the titties,"
something I doubted. In the oven,
the molasses bubbled up in dark, syrupy veins
through the crumbs. As for Betty,
the rumour next week was that our teacher
had called her mother, the difference vanished,
at least to the naked eye:
we all took off our 3-D glasses.

Beverly Ann Lee (1936-2006)

1.

She landed in Edmonton
without a passport or driver's license.
"Ah told the immigration man
Ah was from Texas and came up here
to see my cousin and buy a *mank* coat,"
and he said, "I know you're from Texas, ma'am.'
Now how did he know that?"
"It's your accent, Beverly."
"But I talk exactly like y'all!"

This was the year it didn't snow in Edmonton
till just before New Year's, and the furriers
on Jasper Avenue heard oil wells and Cadillacs
in that accent, when they should have heard
a counselling job and a Honda.
One clerk spread sables on the floor
and told her to walk barefoot on them,
but she thought it wasn't right,
though she had the tiniest feet.

2.

Her parents never stopped complaining
that she'd quit the phone company
to go to college, and her children
liked to refute her arguments
with, "That's mamma's education talking."
The logic was bad but their tone irrefutable.

She kept on studying. The day she got her PhD,
the *Miami Herald* ran a story,
a little human interest item:
"Hard Luck Texan one of NSU's Successes,"
tabulating two open heart surgeries,
three carotid operations, a stroke,
two episodes of heart failure, and a carjacking,
all in the course of her studies.

I would have liked being there
to spread sables for her feet,
and that is the voice of my affection talking.

In Praise of Gravy

For the Southerner, cooking fat
is a sacrament: sometimes
I am mesmerized by the aroma
of the worst kind of fried chicken,
like Kentucky Fried,
which one inspired little boy
called "spitty-up chicken."

Gravy-making is the highest art,
an indissoluble marriage of fat and starch.
A "long gravy" means you make a lot of it,
a "Minnie-cat gravy" is made with milk,
though grown-ups call it sawmill gravy.
"Red-eye gravy" is created from ham
and gets its name from the red oval spot
that forms when the gravy is reduced —
a vegetarian's nightmare.
"Red-eye gravy and biscuits"
is a Southern password, a shibboleth:
say it and you're just whistlin' Dixie.

Did You Ever See Such a Sight

for Leona Gom, Keeper of Mouse Lore

First he'd eat the flour off the peanut butter
then he'd come back the same night
to lick the peanut butter itself
leaving the expensive trap in the corner
ready for any blundering big toe
I came to think of him
as a cat burglar among mice
The heavy winter snows
had sheltered the field mice from predators
so they could spend the winter
eating our garden roots and bulbs
and copulating into a population explosion
that exploded into my kitchen one night
as a single brown individual
Turning on the light I saw him
rushing to hide behind the toaster oven
I made a barricade of chopping boards
and reached into the knife block without looking
and pulled out a long blade
but he suddenly rushed across the counter
with me swinging the knife at him
till he vanished into rodent hyperspace
When I looked at what I held
I saw it was the carving knife
but I knew the mouse wasn't blind
Not with that terrified look
And I was left without even the tip of his tail

Bed and Breakfast

> The world may be divided into people that read, people that
> write, people that think, and fox-hunters.
> — William Shenstone

The bed and breakfast was a listed building,
designed by a Regency architect,
tarted up with a new tennis court
and a power gate for the Range Rover.
Our hostess showed us the rhododendrons
and explained how they spread: the tree
leans forward on its elbows
till it can sink its fingers into the earth.
She was ever-so-genteel,
a blonde of the horsey set: the mantel
in the breakfast room was covered with ribbons
and photographs of the local Hunt.
She deplored the skinheads in camouflage gear
who trail the hunts with rifles, hoping a fox
will bolt past the hounds into their sights.
'With the fox hunting ban, it will come to men like that
culling them at night, catching the poor foxes
in lights and shooting them between the eyes.'

Her husband, a sad man with a broken foot,
sat in the office next to our fine rooms
working at account books.
At night we could hear the wife shrieking
about bills, with a broad accent
slipping through the cracks in her voice.
The poor fox in the woods,
with a wounded paw, baffled in the lights,
waits for the crack of the rifle.

A Duty of Care

> The beast of the field shall honour me, the dragons and the owls: because I give waters in the wilderness, and rivers in the desert.
>
> — Isaiah 43:20

Michael pulled over on the road
between Cork and Dunmanway
to show me where a wild swan
once flew into the power lines
and burst into flames.
He thought he should bury it
and carried it to his car.
How heavy the smoldering body was,
and the current had blown a hole in it.
The path from the fallen swan
to his light switch in Drinagh
was traceable in theory,
Michael thought.
The law of damages
has an inexhaustible phrase,
"to owe a duty of care."

Michael raises barn owls
in tree boxes. The species
grows more and more uncommon.
This morning in Ballydehob
we stood at an Antiques window
where a Wildlife Conservancy poster
showed a barn owl. The caption read,
"Have You Seen This Bird?"
"Yes, I have," Michael said,

pointing to a glass bell
in the same window, holding a specimen
whose only visible flaw was death.
He kept repeating the question
and its answer, "Yes, I have, I have."

The Firebrand River

1.

Looking down the Grand Canyon,
the fundamentalists
with their peculiar squint
see 6,000 years of history.

Looking down the Canyon,
the conquistadors saw a river
about six feet across. Three agile men
struggled part way down and returned
to say that boulders which looked the size of a man
were higher than the great tower of Seville,
and that the river was half a league across,
just as their native guides had told them.

2.

The canyon wren who walked around
our landing place saw the toe of my shoe
and skittered away, still probing
for insects in the crevices of rock.
Famous for its liquidity of song,
the wren subsists without water:
the width of the river is irrelevant.
He didn't sing his descending scales for us.

3.

The Spaniards twisted reason
to call it the Firebrand River,
after the Yuma Indians
who moved naked in the cold nights
with a firebrand to keep warm,
shifting it from one hand to the other.
Looking up the Canyon walls,
we saw the sun setting,
but when our helicopter topped the rim
the sun still had inches to go,
not quite igniting the horizon.

The Gang

Sparrows behave like teenagers,
going everywhere together,
loitering at the bird feeder
their 7-Eleven store.
They see my form at the window
and react as if I were a squad car
pulling into the parking lot:
they fly to the spruce tree,
and tweet without cell phones.

Fast eaters, they spill seed on the snow,
and sometimes descend to peck it.
One keeps trying to helicopter back up
like a hummingbird, but his wings
are visible, a clumsy ventriloquist
whose lips are clearly moving.

Scenes Glimpsed through a BritRail Sandwich

Rick my physiotherapist asked
if I remembered the BritRail sandwiches:
they were always labelled "fresh-cut"
The ham was so thin he said
you could read the newspaper through it
"Do you mean that's a good thing," his assistant asked
"or are you making some kind of joke?"

Hove to London

The tall woman in the black dress
got on with a big empty wicker birdcage
She had black lipstick long black nails
and bare feet approaching black

She sat all the way to London
with the bird cage on her lap
opening and shutting the little door
with a puzzled look on her face
as if she were trying to figure out
how to get into it

Brighton to London

St. Peter said the heavens and earth
would melt with a great fervent heat

Every time the Victoria express
passes the big sign for
WORLD'S END TILES
SILVERTHORNE ROAD
BATTERSEA SW10
I wonder just how hot
they crank up their kilns

Shoreham-by-Sea to Hove

The Bobbie astounded my little boy
by taking off his helmet
removing the two Twix bars
he carried on top of his head
and eating them with great smacking satisfaction

Brighton to London

As for signs I mustn't forget
THE WORSHIPFUL COMPANY OF BASKETMAKERS
just the right stop
for a woman with an empty birdcage

Driving around Cape Sable Island

I thought of the island as a lobster trap,
after I got lost and couldn't find the causeway.
I was a puny morsel of white meat
in the blue painted shell of my rented Ford
a car as awkward as a crustacean. Poor brakes
and slushy steering. How could I get lost on an island?
The yards had stacks of lobster traps.
A half-finished Cape Island boat in a shed
had the hull of Noah's ark
in the old picture books.
At the Baptist church near the sea
the tombstones stood like boundary markers
with lichens on the land side
and salt on the water side.
In front of a house with chickens on the steps
I saw a group of little girls with doll buggies.
Boys chugged up and down the roads on mopeds
and chickens crossing the road for the usual reason
went squawking in terror.
A little further on two girls strolled with a real buggy
and a real baby. I waved to them.
I could see the bridge and I was ready
to show why the tourist crosses the causeway.

A Celestial Symposium

Olga noticed that the bus driver
had a big copy of Schopenhauer
that he read at the tour stops
"How can you read such a bad philosopher?"
"Lady, if you had a banquet in heaven
with Jesus and Socrates and King Solomon
then Schopenhauer could sit right down
and hold his own with them all night"

I find myself imagining Schopenhauer
offering a platter of lamb to Socrates —
"It's not very good but you'll like it anyway"
Socrates wants to know what good really means
Jesus declines the platter with a smile
and hands it on to King Solomon
who complains that no one ever lets him carve

Walter Benjamin Checks into the Kaanapali Hyatt-Regency

Escaped from the Nazis, he became a professor
at Princeton, emeritus now, at 100 the oldest living
Marxist thinker, a silent eminence wheeled in
at conferences. Every speaker acknowledges him,
looks nervously for his inscrutable reaction.
Tracie, the grad student attendant, pushes his chair
around the art in the lobby, one of the finest collections
of Orientalia in private hands. The pleasure dome
of this hotel looks insubstantial, but it's well-capitalized
and amortized. He sees lagoons and islands, nine waterfalls,
and peacocks strolling on lawns that are in the lobby
but open to the stars. The Japanese garden has priceless Buddhas.
Tracie parks his wheelchair at a poolside bar
which manages to be below water and stay dry.
She orders herself one of those slow island drinks,
lots of coconut milk, rum and passionfruit.
The little umbrella lolls in the glass as she flirts with the barman.
Benjamin is still thinking about the statues and the porcelain,
trying to expand his theory of art. He turns up his oxygen.
A mechanical production robs the work of its aura,
its unique presence in time and space.
But these works are real, placed in a South Sea
that never was, and they've lost their aura too.
Where has it gone? He thinks he sees the answer
as Tracie wipes her mouth and slaps her gold card down.
It gleams on the dark bar like Buddha's smile.

A Partial Tour Guide to West Edmonton Mall

> There is not a crevice in the cliff of the established order into which the ironist might hook a fingernail.
> — Theodor Adorno, *Juvenal's Error*

The Mall as everyone in Edmonton calls it is unspeakable, not because it is worse than anything else but because it parodies itself, with its replicas of the Santa Maria and the Crown Jewels of England, its bronze hooker talking perpetually to a metallic cop on Bourbon Street. At The Marketplace Chapel, weary shoppers can lay down their burdens and pray for daily bread and forgiveness of debts.

The homeless live in the miles of corridors behind the stores and store rooms and never appear on the Canada Census. The exotic Australian cockroaches brought into the Mall with the tropical plants for the waterpark live wherever they can but prefer the food carousels. For all their large brains the dolphins in the show tank have expressed no opinions about home. The adolescent mall rats have staked their turf: headbangers, Phase I; rappers, Phase II; punks and alternatives, Phase III. Sociologists and reporters writing them up have lunch at food carousels with the entomologists tracking the cockroaches.

Babies are said to have been born deep in the interior but only a few deaths are recorded: the frogman fixing the submarine ride who caught his arm in machinery and drowned, the riders on the Mindbender roller coaster whose cars came off the track. These accidents were nobody's fault.

Opportunities for *jouissance*: the Fantasyland hotel with its ancient Roman Room (armless couches and marble bath) and the Truck Room with flashing lights and a bunk in the flatbed of a truck. The hookers who occasionally work in RV's in the parking lot are not sanctioned by the management.

The fountains of Versailles, they are called, spout water all day in Phase II. Their white noise accompanies the glitter of chrome and glass creating a synaesthetic zombie potion. I do not think they look much like the fountain I saw in Versailles, where a great bronze chariot of Apollo rises with horses from the spray to figure as Louis the Sun King. Louis wants to visit WEM but hostilities between the Most Christian King and Her Britannic Majesty prevent the visit, which is most unfair when we consider that Hitler got to visit Paris.

Walter Benjamin said that "the methodological relationship between the metaphysical investigation and the historical one is a stocking turned inside out." If I turn this stocking inside out I see Charles Baudelaire's staring face from the famous daguerreotype. Baudelaire strolls up and down the mall after midnight window-shopping and murmuring "greed, lust, pauperism, boredom." Just before dawn he often stares at the bronze hooker until a security guard tells him to move along. He goes past the flagship of Columbus to the Fantasyland Hotel where he meets his mistress, Jeanne Duval, who has been turning tricks in the parking lot. He realizes that irony can get no purchase on the bright surfaces of the Mall but he has no other method.

More Fun than a Barrel of Sea-Monkeys

Nothing to say about Las Vegas that isn't obvious.
Still, I must render unto *Caesars Palace*
that which is Caesar's, and remember two things:
the *Amazing Sea-Monkeys* Slot Machines,
and the man-sized chicken suit — reduced to $129.99 —
at Houdini's Magic Shop on the Grand Canal
inside the Venetian Hotel. The store has a photo
of Michael Jackson's visit. He didn't buy the yellow suit.

I watched the shop from my sidewalk table
at the Trattoria Reggiano. Twirling my fork,
I ate some very good pasta with lemons and capers
as the clerk demonstrated card tricks in his doorway,
treating the deck like a yo-yo. I couldn't see any wires.
Above me, a blue sky with shapely clouds that never moved.

Uncle Ned Says Grace

Uncle Ned was a retired sailor
with an innocent gift for swearing
One day at dinner saying the grace
he went on so long that Aunt Jill
walked about ladling the stew into bowls
After he mumbled his way into asking
"How the fuck can we pay the rising taxes, Lord?"
she hit him on the back of the head
with the big iron spoon
and he murmured "sorry"
before resuming
his petitions and beseechings
to the Skipper on the Celestial Quarterdeck

I had to reassess *Treasure Island*:
maybe the pirates meant no impiety
when they sent Billy Bones the Black Spot
cut out of the cover of a Bible

Reading the Entrails

> I defy augury.
> — Hamlet

I surmise that the hostess
wants to balance her social books
by having her husband's acquaintances over
for a no-fuss barbecue. The other couple
are suspicious of any food they don't grow
in their front yard. The man, a classics scholar,
has spent his career trying to reconstruct
the Roman technique of haruspication,
prophetic reading of entrails. He's brought chicken
from the illegal flock they keep in the back yard.
He doesn't smile when I tell him
that Francis Bacon died of pneumonia
after stuffing the cavity of a chicken with snow
in a primitive refrigeration experiment.
"I spend a lot of time with warm chicken guts,"
he says as solemnly as a Roman augur.
I wonder what qualified me for this party.

The host has just burnt his beard
and eyebrows lighting the gas barbecue.
I don't know if I want to eat the chicken.

The scholar complains that his neighbors
leave threatening notes in the mail
and have cut the wires of their many wind chimes.
His wife tells us that they sleep
in separate bedrooms, she with their daughter,
he with the son, except at the new moon.

The hostess has botched the dessert, a cake
that never solidified. My wife tells her
to spoon it up and call it pudding.
It's a great success except with me:
I see singed hairs of the host's beard in my bowl.

Scenes from a Divorce

How could he tell the counsellor
that his chief complaint
was waking in the night to hear
his wife sucking her thumb?
That would demean him as well as her.

His father's superstition:
eat pork before you fall asleep
and wake with the face of a pig.
Every time he slept with the other woman
he'd wake up and rub his face
feeling for a snout.
When the counsellor said this meant
he didn't respect women
he thought she was stupid.

His wife liked it when he worked on his telescope
in the nude, walking around the Pyrex mirror
with the ceramic grinder, eight or nine steps
each circuit. He did wear a bandanna
to keep the abrasive powder
out of his mouth and nose. She said
he looked like a bandit.

His velvet painting of a bandido
with the sombrero, the stubbly beard
and the red-tipped cigar was meant to be camp.
But the Christ Crowned with Thorns
was a serious gift from his parents
that he couldn't take down
yet didn't want to leave up.

She never learned to ride a bicycle
so she made him sell his
and buy a tandem machine.
He had to steer and she barely pedaled.
When he left they couldn't divide the bike.
It was easy enough
to take the bandido to the other woman's house.
He left Christ in the living room
and the unfinished telescope
in the garage next to the bicycle.

The Eyewitness

I watched *The Longest Day* at the Days Inn Motel
the night of June sixth, in a room
where the lamp was too faint for reading.

The movie was mostly bloodless,
and the most terrifying scenes told the story
of Pvt. John Steele, the paratrooper
who spent his longest day dangling from a steeple
in the burning village of St. Mère-Église
with the bells ringing non-stop. He saw his friends
die in the streets. Villagers recalled "the dead soldier,"
an Oscar-worthy performance. Helpless, he watched
the true newsreel of the war cranking through his mind,
a patron saint of eyewitnesses, sanctified
by the purity of his interest,
a holiness denied to us, the commandos
of the remote control. In real life,
he didn't remember the bells ringing.
In the movie, he was deaf when the rescuers came,
the extras led by swaggering movie stars.

The Passionate Haystack

From the ellipse machine at the health club
I watched *The Antiques Road Show*.
The old man on the screen, the son
of a British judge at Nuremberg,
was showing off his souvenirs:
the Union Jack from the courtroom,
the photos of the defendants.
He got to listen through headphones,
German into English. The spectators
called one blonde woman in the dock
"The Passionate Haystack,"
from the days when her hair was uncombed.
On others it was tamed into a *Veronica*,
the peek-a-boo bangs named for a movie star.

Skiing and rowing at the same time,
I was the spectator of a spectator,
my sweat representing no passion at all.

Everyone attending the trials
made daily bets on the woman's hair,
he said. The steady odds were 6:4
for the haystack. He recalled the K-rations
he got as a member of the judge's party:
after the shortages in England,
the two Hershey bars and four cigarettes
were deep luxury, "the kind of thing the Americans
were known for." That was the time of his life:
history in simultaneous translation, cigarettes
and chocolate, and a glamorous defendant
in the dock, her odds of hanging
about a hundred to one.

Three Birdsongs

Masterclass, Vienna, 1784

Mozart's starling could whistle the theme
from the last movement of his Piano Concerto
No. 17. But it did sing the G natural as a G sharp.

Das war schön, he wrote in his expense book.
Always praise the beginner.

When the bird died, Mozart made his friends
dress in black and march solemnly
to the tiny grave, where he read a bad poem
in honour of the student he named "Star Vogel."

Serenade, Oxted, Surrey, 1924

Beatrice Harrison sat in a ditch with her cello,
wearing her best clothes to get in a concertizing mood.
She was trying to lure the nightingale near her cottage
to sing live for the BBC. Maybe it was stage fright
or the technicians with their ton of equipment,
but it was almost an hour before the bird
joined in for "Danny Boy," singing in thirds.

Das war auch schön.

Solemn Vespers, Oxted, Surrey, 1942

Beatrice had moved away, but the annual concerts
continued, with a nightingale a cappella. This time
the archival recording carries a ground bass,
the roar of 197 bombers on the way to Mannheim.
The flip side caught the bird hours later,
still singing as 186 of them returned,
many pounds lighter.
      Das war nicht schön.

Hawthornden Hours

This is a poet's castle, not a soldier's.
The triangle of gun loops above the gate
was a whimsy in 1638. There were no sieges here.
From my bath I look through the skylight
at the weather vane on the conical turret.
The letters have been lost, so I can tell
which way the wind blows without naming it.

The old sycamore where William Drummond
met Ben Jonson has turned to a stump
with a young sycamore growing in it.
The arms of Drummond over the entrance
have weathered till they're indecipherable.
Still, the hours pass so gently here
and in such ceremonious order
that the true emblem of the place
is the sundial speckled with lichens
which has fallen over by a bank of daffodils.

Bombay Sapphire

We knew an ex-flight attendant who liked to say, "Pour me a double, I hate to fly on only one wing." That was before she took the silver wings of Trans-Canada Airlines off her lapel and married a construction king. They practiced philanthropy with open hands, and I drink a toast to them in the garden, where I poured triples from the gin bottle by mistake. I confess that three wings leave us spinning. I spot a black feather from a magpie caught in the kale that grows in an old cream separator. Bumblebees are dithering between the pale blue flowers of the oregano and bright yellow blossoms of the St. John's Wort. *Uppers and downers*, Olga says. They aren't much interested in the huge Casablanca lilies, which makes us wonder what the fragrance is for, except to intoxicate the gardeners. Bombay Sapphire in its blue-tinted bottle has ten botanicals, among them, angel root and grains of paradise. A four-winged bumblebee in staggering flight lands on the lip of a foxglove blossom, then crawls into Eden.

Portobello Road Market

1. *Shop*

With agoraphobia piled on jetlag
we sheltered from the crowds
in a little antique store where you were smitten
and I wanted a small painting on glass
inspired by Martin de Vos's
"Allegory of the Four Continents":
a blonde woman in a feathered headdress
bow in one hand, tomahawk in the other
all pastels and gentle curves
but seated side-saddle on a giant caiman
Amérique sauvage in the rococo style

2. *Leda*

The detachment of jetlag let me see
the strangeness of that small ivory
stripped of the classical aura:
the swan riding a woman
wrapping her in his wings
Such ravishing violence
cut from the tusk of an elephant

Venus in Edinburgh

National Gallery of Scotland

Roman Bronze

On loan from Naples,
this Latin nude
with a Greek accent
isn't rising from the sea
in triumph. No, after millennia
encased in the ashes of Vesuvius,
Venus needs her bath.
Poised on one foot,
she reaches to remove a sandal,
beauty clothing herself
in nakedness.

Venus Anadyomene

She stands waist high in water
and her soft skin tones
help us distinguish the blue
of the sea from the blue of the sky.
With both hands she slowly twists the water
from her rope of long brown hair.
The little scallop shell floating
next to her must be Titian's homage
to Botticelli. A goddess could never
have ridden on this bath toy.
She will have better playthings.

Degas Bronze

A Venus-for-Hire was hired
to model a reclining bather
whose sea shell is a round tub
about the size of a hand basin.
The image was born from wax,
not the Paphian sea foam,
and it took shape under the fingers
of a celibate artist with failing eyesight.

What languorous movements
set the bronze water rippling?

The French Bed

Rembrandt, Etching and drypoint, 1646

The canopy has been pulled back, revealing the lovers:
they haven't taken off their clothes, but the posture
is unmistakable, her knees raised and parted,
and he lying between them. She is smiling
and holds his waist with both hands,
but the artist has left a third arm from a prior version
lying on the sheets in post-coital languor.
A bed-post holds his plumed cap, and the wine glass
sitting on a little table transcends the tattered adage:
half empty and half full at the same time.

Aelbert Cuyp: River Landscape with Horseman and Peasants

> Time hath, my lord, a wallet at his back
> Wherein he puts alms for oblivion
> — William Shakespeare, *Troilus and Cressida*

1.

The rider has stopped to ask directions of a herdsman
who points the way in a landscape with Dutch cows
and German mountains, back-lit with Italian sunlight.
Cuyp had seen the mountains but made them higher.
Perhaps one direction would be as true as another
in this picture, but the herdsman is pointing west,
if we can believe the afternoon sun.

2.

My premium-plus photo paper is good for a century,
the package tells me, a claim I cannot test.
If I tucked the receipt into the album
for my heirs, its ink would fade faster than the pictures.

3.

The leaves in Cuyp's picture are fading:
the pigment came from petals of Dyer's Rocket
and has proved unstable. The inorganic colours
hold steady. Near the lower left corner,
a kneeling hunter in the shadow of a bush
aims his long-barrelled flintlock at five swimming ducks.
The hammer will never fall, the game bag will stay empty.
In the other corner, the artist's name, *A cuip*.
Near the painted letters, the burdock leaves
are signed: *Time, His Mark*.

The Art of Painting

Jan Vermeer, Kunsthistorisches Museum, Vienna

A blue and gold tapestry has been swept aside
and held by a chair. The painter sits at the easel,
facing away from us, dressed in black,
with the kind of slashed doublet called
a "simpleton" because the white undershirt shows.
The model in her blue dress is Clio, muse of history.
She stands in profile with a slender trumpet in her right hand
and a heavy yellow book in the left, symbols of fame.
Crowned with laurel, she looks down at music on a table,
and doesn't quite see the white mask beside it,
an out-sized human face. History is the map on the wall,
Claez Visscher's image of the Netherlands before civil war
ripped them in half. Vermeer has put a modest crease
in the map to mark the change. So far, the canvas on the easel
has only a few laurel leaves. The painter's hand,
resting on a maul stick, paints them blue instead of green.
The picture was bought by Hitler, a connoisseur
whose vocation was tearing maps to pieces.
When the bombers came too close to Berchtesgaden,
he had this gem of his collection hidden in a salt mine
to shelter it from the turmoil of history,
but he kept the manuscript of Wagner's *Rienzi*
with him in the bunker, where it perished.
Later his corpse was incinerated in a bomb crater
along with his dead wife and two dogs,
a malign Siegfried immolated with retainers.
See the painter's hand, crowned with blue laurel.

Entering Paradise

Lucas Cranach der Älterer, Der Jungbrunnen, 1546
Anonym Niederlande, Die Himmelfahrt Cristi, c. 1520

In Lucas Cranach the Elder's "Fountain of Youth,"
the old women come, hobbling, slumped on horseback,
loaded into wagons, carried on litters, piggyback on old men,
one even pushed along in a wheelbarrow by an old man.
Each is examined by a doctor in a red gown and disrobed
by his female assistant before entering a pool
presided over by a columnar fountain topped
by statues of Venus and Cupid. The eye follows bathers
steadily younger going from left to right. My favorite
scrubs her hair in a stream from the fountain.
The water has turned all the grey heads to strawberry blonde.

Climbing out, naked nymphs are ushered by a cavalier
into a scarlet tent to change into fine gowns.
In the background of the picture, ladies and gentleman
feast, dance, or stroll under trees bearing indistinct fruits.
The picture is a favorite in plastic surgeons' brochures,
but I saw it in the Berlin Gemäldegalerie.
A German woman standing beside me laughed out loud
and I said to her, *Wo dieses Bad ist?* As we chuckled together,
a whirring sound approached from behind. We turned
to see an elderly woman in a motorized wheelchair
approaching the painting, her hand a claw on the lever.

Decency said to move on before she saw the picture,
and I shuffled off to the Netherlandish "Ascension"
on the same wall, with its cluster of figures looking up in wonder
toward the top of the canvas, where nothing of Christ is visible
except for his feet protruding from the hem of a blue robe
as he perpetually rises and rises into heaven.

Treasures of the Green Vault. Dresden

> Objects which in themselves we view with pain, we delight
> to contemplate when reproduced with minute fidelity.
> — Aristotle

August the Strong of Saxony
was the father of his country
in the most literal way,
with 365 illegitimate children,
which must have meant jokes about leap year.
His other nickname was "the Saxon Hercules,"
after his gift for snapping horseshoes with his hands,
but he collected the most fragile Chinese porcelains
and once traded a regiment of dragoons
to Frederick I of Prussia
for one hundred fifty-one Kangxi vases,
one for every four men.
Not a very loving father.

A few years later, Frederick's alchemist
fled to Saxony after a gold-making fiasco.
He created white gold for August
by working out the secret of porcelain
in a fortress laboratory at Meissen.

Grown richer, August could stuff his treasure vault
with delicate objects, like hexahedrons of ivory
whose sides look like fine lace, and the little figures
of the Huguenot jeweller, Jean Louis Girardet,
who specialized in beggars and maimed soldiers,
enamelled and set with jewels.
The vault has Girardet's blind man
led by a boy and the dwarf
dressed smartly in a dragoon's uniform.

The masterpiece is a crippled veteran
on an ivory base with diamonds and pearls.
He extends a deep hat for alms,
bowing as well as a man with a crutch can bow.
His wooden leg is purest gold and beautifully worked.

August the Strong died of a gangrenous toe,
and we might squint at that fact
with a jeweller's glass of irony,
but it won't touch him in the grave.

The Demonstrators

Stoke-on-Trent

Lynne Hooper, China Painter, Royal Doulton

She can tell left from right-handed painters
and always knows if a figurine
was painted by a woman or a man.
She explains the gender differences
in china painters as she makes strokes
with a fine brush, precise as a surgeon's blade.
"The women hold the figurines as they paint,
men always improvise something to skewer
the hollow figure on, painting at a distance.
They start at the bottom and work up,
while women begin with the head.
Men give particular care to the bosom
of a female doll, but women Max-Factor the face."
She is painting Anna of the Five Towns,
in the Arnold Bennet Series. Lynne is
a woman of the Towns herself, a brunette
with a little stroke of white at each temple.

Roy Yates, Engraver, Wedgwood

> Line engraving has a curious quality of metallic hardness and austere precision. . . .
>
> *The Oxford Companion to Art*

"Rack of eye, that's all you've got,"
the white-haired man tells us in his dry tone.
"Have you never heard that expression?"
He puts down the copper plate and frames his eyes
with raised forefingers, marking the ends
of an imaginary ruler. "It means the measurements
are all made by sight." He is working on
the engraving for a blue willow bowl.
The fluid lines of the picture take form
as tiny dots from the stipple punch, tapped
with a hammer. His favorite punch has worn
to half its size in thirty years. Nothing matters
but the point, the locus of penetration.
The punch will outlast the man himself.
This is an oatmeal bowl: the flat collar of rim
is the hardest part of the pattern.
He must prepare the abstract border
of circles and squares by punching out
ellipses and lozenges. They will flatten
into their true shapes, just as the tiny dots
in the bottom will blur into inky lines:
the undulant willow, the waves of river.
The bridge and the three men crossing it
with tiny boxes are the Stoke variant
on a Japanese copy of a Chinese pattern.
Nothing is original, nothing is the same.
How to judge the distortions that make a pattern
run true? "Only rack of eye, that's all, rack of eye."

Wedding Cakes and Buddhas

Fiona Kinsella, The New Gallery
14th Century Tibetan, Glenbow Museum

A conservator's nightmare, the exhibit
of wedding cakes in clear boxes:
real fondant shapes resting on mats of human hair,
with trimmings like silver-plated baby spoons,
kewpie dolls, cartridge cases, dental picks,
real human teeth, animal fangs, bones,
locks of hair from women, from men,
from a stranger of unknown sex,
and the customary white sugar roses.
What about hair of the dog that bit you,
I want to ask, but the artist isn't here.
One fossilized bison bone sticks out of a cake
with the epiphysis — the knobbly end —
on top, looking like the revolving crown
of the Calgary Tower.
The Glenbow is almost
in the shadow of the Tower, and its top floor
has two rooms of Oriental art. The Buddhas
share space with the copulating or fighting
Hindu gods. One statue of Kali
tramples out a wedding-dance on the corpse
of her bridegroom. Across the room,
there's a Buddha in the lotus position.

The Hindu deities embody everything
that he rejected. His perfection —
copper alloy plated with flawless gold —
seems to deny the doctrine
of impermanence. The conservators
found a rose bud nestled in his lap,
preserved for centuries by the dry thin air
of Tibet, a fragile decoration
on the wedding cake of Nirvana.

The Lorelei

> I don't know what it could mean
> For me to feel so sad;
> There's a tale from ancient times
> That I can't get out of my mind.
> — Heinrich Heine

At High Styles I wait with a towel on my shoulders
while Kurt trims the elderly woman in the next chair.
She talks about her sister, Elsa, who just died from
Alzheimer's:
"The doctor said when the appetite centre is destroyed,
there's no hope, you die in a month or two."
A buyer from the library is coming to inspect Elsa's books,
mostly old poetry. "I can't read much in German anymore,
it makes me very tired." Kurt begins to quote Schiller,
a long poem he learned in *hochschule* just after the war.
I once had to memorize "Die Lorelei," Heine's lyric
about the Rhine witch who lured sailors to the rocks.
During Hitler's time, the poem stayed in print —
with no mention of its Jewish author — as a "German folksong."
The woman wonders if her sister's books are valuable.
Most of them are printed in the old blackletter script.

Her haircut finished, the woman gets up slowly
and unfolds her walker, then begins the long trip
to the door. I figure the riddle of the Sphinx
needs rewriting now: *What walks on four legs
in the morning, two at noon, and six at night?*
I remember that as the Lorelei on her rocks
sang that bewitching song, she combed out
her own golden hair with a golden comb,
and that thought makes me strangely sad.

Unfinished Symphony

1.

On my hospital window someone has painted
a circle of flower pots as a child would paint them
to hold a motto by Ralph Waldo Emerson:
"Trust Thyself: every heart vibrates to that iron string."
I don't mind Emerson's self-help medicine,
but I have heard an iron string plucked all night
by the screaming man with dementia next door —
sometimes a siren building with each repetition,
sometimes the howl of an animal in the woods,
or the shriek of a child with a finger slammed in a door;
just once the scream of a roller coaster drop —
half terror and half joy — and then the siren again.
At Longfellow's funeral, the elderly Emerson asked,
"Where are we? What house? Who is the sleeper?"

2.

The monitor on the Vital Signs trolley
beeps twice for each temperature reading.

The synthetic sounds are precisely the opening notes
of the first theme from Schubert's eighth symphony,
the notes that enter after the dark warnings
from the cellos and basses.
I hear the cart approaching, pausing next door,
then pealing the intervals
that lay for forty years in the dust
of a Vienna attic.
Schubert left the symphony unfinished,
and he was finished at thirty-two,
close to half my age.

Is there anyone on this corridor
who wants to conclude at any span?
The cart is rolling closer,
now turning into my room.
As the machine records my body's heat,
I add in my mind
the rest of Schubert's theme,
the brave oboe and the confident clarinet
that brighten the dark wanderings in the lower register.

Jessica Williams at the Yardbird Suite

William Blake saw the soul of his brother Robert
ascend into heaven clapping its hands.

At the jazz club, Jessica Williams played a song
in memory of her cat. At the break,
you told her about our own cat, Hercules,
shuddering and collapsing with a saddle thrombosis.
Williams held Olga's hands with her own,
that famous wide span, and described
how she felt her cat's energy leave its body,
rising through the ceiling.

Holding Hercules at the vet,
I felt him twitch once,
very slightly, as the needle entered.

In the second set, Williams played a number
with notes so glassy they might have broken,
then kicked it into stride piano. After, we were the ones
who ascended into heaven, clapping our hands.

Aboard the *Twin Star Rocket*

The Texas farmer came back from Chicago
with a legend for Lamar County.
The man next to him on the train
was as familiar as Chaplin or Gandhi.
As the night progressed
curiosity grew, and the question needed to be asked:
"Excuse me sir, are you Dr. Einstein?"
"Yes, I am," came the answer.
They had almost reached Kansas City,
where the farmer would change for Dallas,
so he had to find something to say,
but all that he could manage was,
"Say, professor, would you like a beer?"
Einstein smiled and said no.
I imagine the tired conductor
checking his Hamilton watch,
and the great headlamp shining into the night
with a constant velocity,
whatever the speed of the train.

Astral Journey

I had to drive by night from Vancouver to Jasper
From Hope I took the Yellowhead —
the dark highway with hardly a road sign
I counted on a Vancouver classic rock station
to keep me awake, with whole albums from 1968
— *Electric Ladyland* and *Beggars Banquet* —
played without a break at 100,000 watts

But at my sleepiest point
the DJ put on Van Morrison's *Astral Weeks*
45 minutes of dreamy mysticism
a tranquilizer dart between the eyes
If I ventured in the slipstream
between the viaducts of your dream
backed with quiet jazz
— guitar, bass, flute, and vibes —
and a string quartet overdubbed
We are goin' up to heaven
We are goin' to heaven
but a ditch is a bad shortcut to the hereafter:
a viaduct of nightmare where the silver cord snaps
and the cords of all the amps unplug

You breathe out you breathe in you breathe out
And you're high on your high-flyin' cloud
Wrapped up in your magic shroud
Ah the quiet footsteps of the walking bass
when I needed *In-a-Gadda-da Vida* or *Wheels of Fire*
I could make out the first mountains in growing light
as the signal faded and I was safe
The radio static kept me awake —
foam spun off the carrier wave

Along the Queen Elizabeth II Highway

I like the robot on a treadmill outside the Flaman factory.
Usually he wears a Superman suit but lately he's Spiderman.
He keeps going in the coldest weather and gets dressed like
    Santa at Christmas.
He must long for a new job, maybe crashing cars into barriers.

Surely he makes a new trinity with Sisyphus and Atlas.
Sisyphus has the best of it, with time for a smoke on the way down,
but Atlas just stands like a weightlifter frozen in an overhead jerk.

After all these years, the Flaman robot isn't a millimetre closer to
    Calgary.

Open Books

1.

The two movers carried the furniture
past the book open on the reading stand
in the hallway. As he waited for me to sign
the bill of lading, the one in charge said,
"You people must be very religious, having
that big Bible right in the front hall."
"No, it's the works of Shakespeare."
He took a close look, "Hey, Bobby,
Shakespeare wrote about you and me,
right here: *A Comedy of Errors*."

2.

Dodie put ice water on the cane table
in the sun porch for the immigrant roofers.
She came upon the three of them
standing at the table, twisting their necks
to look at the open pages of the book
she'd left lying there: *The Satanic Verses*.
They hadn't touched the forbidden pages,
but they looked up at her, guilt-stricken,
then went back outside to their bubbling
hot-tar machine. The reading from Shakespeare
for this occasion is from *Love's Labour's Lost*:
"I am toiling in a pitch, pitch that defiles."

Eastern Pennsylvania on Flag Day

June 14, 2007

> Where one can no longer love, one should pass by.
> — Friedrich Nietzsche

1.

Mostly I get the American news
mediated by the BBC World Report.
Sometimes a war story reminds me of the 60s,
sets me choking like an asthmatic reacting
to the ozone from a distant lightning strike.

I recall the flag code we learned in school:
the flag must be lowered at night,
and folded into a triangle
in a prescribed pattern.
It can be flown upside down
only as a sign of distress.
An old flag must be burned in a dignified ceremony.
People have been sent to jail
for wearing flag patches
on the seat of their pants.
It used to accompany the slogan
on bumper stickers: America, love it or leave it.

My father's coffin was covered with a flag
that was folded correctly
by the leader of the honour guard.
My mother lost it in one of her moves,
the one flag I would have cherished.

2.

The flags were everywhere in Pennsylvania,
every business, half the houses on any block,
the bumper stickers. In flower beds,
people use them as borders
like red, white and blue flowers.
I even saw traditional barn stars
in the same colour scheme.
On Flag Day, banners broke out like a rash.

I preferred my daughter's rainbow flag
on her porch near Allentown: it has more colours.

Days of -39

When I got my job in Canada,
the buzz in the graduate lounge grew very loud.

"You'll have to teach in an academic gown."

"It will be very cold there —
you can lose your life emptying the garbage."

"No, Alberta is one of the maritime provinces,
he'll get the Gulf Stream!"

The friendly immigration officer at Coutts
kept calling the country "Khanada."
"I think you'll like it very much
in Khanada." Handing over
the landed-immigrant card, he said,
"Welcome to Khanada"
I thought, I can manage the gown
and maybe I'll toughen up for the cold,
but I will never learn to say Khanada.

I arrived in time for the coldest winter
on record in Edmonton, days of -39.
I've never worn a gown,
never heard anyone say Khanada,
and I'm still waiting for the Gulf Stream.

Zones of Hardiness

A visitor from down south stared at my apple tree
and said, "Those don't grow here, you know. It's too cold."
If the apricot tree in Highlands knew it couldn't live there,
it might stop scattering white blossoms over three lawns.
Daffodil bulbs that we planted in old wash tubs
came up in the dark garage this March,
raising their yellow flags in a delusion of spring.
We were too tactful to correct them,
but the visitor, the visitor got apple pie for dessert.

Acknowledgements

ARC, Ariel, Event, Grain, JCT: An International Journal of Curriculum Studies, Lines Review, Matrix, Nashwaak Review, Northern Light, Prairie Fire, Quadrant, Spire Poetry Posters, The Society, Vallum, Wascana Review.

"Zones of Hardiness" appeared on Edmonton Transit Buses as part of the "Take the Poetry Route" series.

Anthologies:

"A Duty of Care" appeared in *ReGreen: New Canadian Ecological Poetry* (Your Scrivener Press, 2009)

"In Praise of Gravy" was published in *New Texas 1995*, and "The Cracking Tower" appeared in *New Texas 1999* (Texas Center for Writers Press).

"Days of -39" and "Eastern Pennsylvania on Flag Day" first appeared in *Crossing Lines: Poets Who Came to Canada in the Vietnam War Era*, edited by Allan Briesmaster and Steven Michael Berzensky (Seraphim Editions, 2008).

"Jessica Williams at the Yardbird Suite," "Waiting for the Gulf Stream," and "Open Books" first appeared in *Waiting for the Gulf Stream*, a pamphlet published by the Olive Reading Series.

Some of these poems were written when I was an International Writing Fellow at Hawthornden Castle. Others were written with the assistance of a writing grant from the Alberta Foundation for the Arts. The poems have benefited from the comments of John Reibetanz, Olga Costopoulos, Meli Costopoulos, Shawna Lemay, Michael Penny, Lee Elliott, Kimmy Beach, Iman Mersal, and Michael McCarthy. I owe a great deal to my mentor, Robert Burlingame. I am grateful for the editorial guidance of Allan Safarik and Paul Wilson.

Bert Almon was born in Port Arthur, Texas in 1943 during a hurricane. He claims to have lived a fairly quiet life since. He completed a BA at the University of Texas at El Paso in 1965 and a PhD at the University of New Mexico in 1971. He came to Canada to teach at the University of Alberta in 1968 and has become a Canadian citizen. He teaches creative writing, modern literature, and autobiography. He won the Writer's Guild of Alberta Award for Poetry in 1998 for *Earth Prime* (Brick Books). He has been a Hawthornden Fellow in Poetry and a finalist in the Blackwell's *Times Literary Supplement* Poetry Competition. His critical works include a study of the Southern US novelist William Humphrey (University of Texas Press), and a book on Texas autobiographies, *This Stubborn Self* (TCU Press, 2002). One of Alberta's best-loved poets, Bert Almon lives in Edmonton with his wife, the poet Olga Costopoulos. *Waiting for the Gulf Stream* is his eleventh collection of poetry.